NO EGG
ON YOUR FACE!

Easy and Delicious Egg-free Recipes
for Kids With Allergies

by **KATRINA JORGENSEN**

CONSULTANT
Amy Durkan MS, RDN, CDN
Nutrition Research Manager
Mount Sinai Medical Center
New York, NY, USA

raintree
a Capstone company — publishers for children

Raintree is an imprint of Capstone Global Library Limited, a company incorporated in
England and Wales having its registered office at 264 Banbury Road, Oxford, OX2 7DY –
Registered company number: 6695582

www.raintree.co.uk
myorders@raintree.co.uk

Edited by Anna Butzer
Designed by Heidi Thompson
Picture research by Morgan Walters
Production by Kathy McColley

ISBN 978 1 4747 1069 5 (hardback)
20 19 18 17 16
10 9 8 7 6 5 4 3 2 1

ISBN 978 1 4747 1074 9 (paperback)
21 20 19 18 17
10 9 8 7 6 5 4 3 2 1

British Library Cataloguing in Publication Data
A full catalogue record for this book is available from the British Library.

Design Elements
Shutterstock: avian, design element, Katerina Kirilova, design element, Lena Pan, design
element, Marco Govel, design element, mexrix, design element, Sabina Pittak, design
element, STILLFX, design element, swatchandsoda, design element

Photography by Capstone Studio: Karon Dubke

Editor's note:
Capstone cannot ensure that any food is allergen-free. The only way to be sure a food is
safe is to read all labels carefully, every time. Cross-contamination is also a risk for those
with food allergies. Please phone food companies to make sure their manufacturing
processes avoid cross-contamination. Also, always make sure you clean hands, surfaces
and tools before cooking.

Printed in the United Kingdom.

CONTENTS

WHAT IS A FOOD ALLERGY?

Our bodies are armed with immune systems. It's the immune system's job to fight infections, viruses and invaders. Sometimes the immune system identifies a particular food as one of these invaders and attacks it. While our immune system fights, a chemical response is triggered and causes an allergic reaction. Reactions vary greatly from a mild skin irritation to having trouble breathing. Whenever you feel you are having a reaction, tell an adult immediately.

The best way to avoid having an allergic reaction is to be aware of what you are eating. Be careful not to consume that allergen. If you are not sure if that allergen is in a food, ask an adult or read the ingredients label of the food container before eating. Unfortunately, allergens can sometimes be hard to identify in an ingredient list. Have a look at www.foodallergy.org/allergens/egg-allergy for a full list of hidden egg terms.

Avoiding food allergens can be hard to do, especially when they are found in so many of our favourite foods. This cookbook will take you on a culinary journey to explore many of the dishes you've had to avoid because of an egg allergy.

Kitchen safety

A safe kitchen is a fun kitchen! Always start your recipes with clean hands, surfaces and tools. Wash your hands and any tools you may use in future steps of a recipe, especially when handling raw meat. Make sure you have an adult nearby to help you with any task you don't feel comfortable doing, such as cutting vegetables or carrying hot pans.

ALLERGY ALERTS AND TIPS

Have other food allergies? No problem.
Have a look at the list at the end of each recipe
for substitutions for other common allergens.
Look out for other cool tips and ideas too!

CONVERSIONS

1/4 teaspoon	1.25 grams or millilitres
1/2 teaspoon	2.5 g or mL
1 teaspoon	5 g or mL
1 tablespoon	15 g or mL
10 grams	1/3 ounce
50 grams	1 3/4 oz
100 grams	3 1/2 oz
455 grams	16 oz (1 pound)
10 mL	1/3 fluid oz
50 mL	1 3/4 fl oz
100 mL	3 1/2 fl oz

Fahrenheit (°F)	Celsius (°C)
325°	160°
350°	180°
375°	190°
400°	200°
425°	220°
450°	230°

THE NO-EGG SCRAMBLE

Eggs are a staple in many breakfast
foods. But you can create a unique
take on a classic early morning meal
by using protein-packed chickpeas.
You'll want to scramble to make this
delicious breakfast entree!

Preparation time: 5 minutes

Cooking time: 10 minutes

Serves 1

Ingredients

30 grams chickpea flour

60 millilitres water

¼ teaspoon salt

¼ teaspoon paprika

¼ teaspoon garlic powder

1 tablespoon olive oil

Tools

small bowl

measuring spoons/scales/jug

whisk

non-stick frying pan

spatula

Allergens eradicated!

No major food allergens found here.

1. Combine the chickpea flour, water, salt, paprika and garlic powder in a small bowl. Whisk ingredients until mixed well. Set aside.

2. Add the olive oil to the frying pan and put on the hob set to medium heat.

3. Add the flour mixture to the frying pan when the olive oil is hot. The oil will appear to ripple a bit when it is ready.

4. Allow to cook for about three minutes, or until the edges begin to bubble.

5. Use a spatula to break up the batter into bite-sized pieces. Continue to cook until the batter is cooked through, approximately another two to three minutes.

6. Remove from heat and serve immediately.

CHEF'S TIP

Include your favourite veggies or toppings such as mushrooms, spinach, peppers or onions. Add them to the frying pan after step 3.

BLUEBERRY BREAD

You don't need eggs to make fluffy, rich bread. Plump and juicy blueberries add a punch of flavour and antioxidants to this freshly baked loaf. Start your day with a sweet blueberry treat!

Preparation time: 15 minutes

Cooking time: 1 hour

Makes 1 loaf

Ingredients

cooking spray

250 grams plain flour

1 teaspoon bicarbonate of soda

1 teaspoon kosher salt

80 millilitres oil, such as olive oil

3 ripe bananas

170 grams granulated sugar

1 teaspoon vanilla extract

150 grams thawed frozen blueberries

Tools

loaf tin

2 mixing bowls

measuring spoons/scales/jug

wooden spoon

fork

toothpick

1. Preheat oven to 160°C. Coat the loaf tin generously with the cooking spray and set aside.

2. Combine the flour, bicarbonate of soda and salt in a mixing bowl. Stir well and set aside.

3. Combine the oil, bananas, sugar and vanilla extract in a second mixing bowl. Using a fork, mash the bananas and mix until they are mostly smooth.

4. Add the banana mixture into the flour mixture. Stir gently until the wet ingredients fully absorb the flour.

5. Pour in the blueberries and stir a few times.

6. Transfer the batter into the greased loaf tin. Then place the tin in the oven for about 45 to 50 minutes. The bread is done when a toothpick inserted into the centre comes out clean.

7. Allow to cool for 10 to 15 minutes before slicing and serving. Store leftovers by covering completely for up to one week.

Allergen alert!

If you need to avoid wheat, use a wheat-free flour blend instead of plain flour.

CHEF'S TIP

Transform your loaf into easy on-the-go snacks by making muffins! Instead of using a loaf tin, fill a muffin tray with paper cases. Scoop the batter into each cup, leaving about one-third of each cup empty at the top. Bake for 30 to 35 minutes.

APPLE SAUCE WAFFLES

Crispy on the outside, fluffy on the inside, these waffles allow you to skip the eggs without compromising the delicious taste. Dive into the flavours of autumn with these sweetly spiced waffles drizzled with maple syrup!

Preparation time: 10 minutes

Cooking time: 5 minutes

Serves 4

Ingredients

500 grams plain flour

1 tablespoon baking powder

¼ teaspoon kosher salt

55 grams granulated sugar

¼ teaspoon ground cinnamon

480 millilitres water

130 grams apple sauce

¼ teaspoon maple extract

60 millilitres oil, such as olive oil

cooking spray

maple syrup, for serving

Tools

2 mixing bowls

measuring spoons/scales/jug

wooden spoon

waffle iron

fork

1. Combine the flour, baking powder, salt, sugar and cinnamon in a mixing bowl. Set aside.

2. Combine the water, apple sauce, maple extract and oil in a second mixing bowl. Stir until well blended.

3. Pour the wet ingredients into the bowl of dry ingredients and mix well.

4. Warm up the waffle iron and spray lightly with cooking spray.

5. Pour a portion of batter into the centre of the iron (it should fill three-quarters of the iron) and close the lid. Follow the recommended cooking time given by the waffle iron brand, or cook until golden brown.

6. Remove from waffle iron with a fork. Repeat steps 4 and 5 until all the batter is used.

7. Serve hot with maple syrup.

TROPICAL GREEK
YOGURT PARFAIT

Who needs eggs for protein! Jump-start your day with an energy-boosting breakfast. With layers of Greek yogurt and crunchy coconut, this parfait is a protein powerhouse!

Preparation time: 5 minutes

Makes 1 parfait

Ingredients

280 grams plain Greek yogurt

2 teaspoons pure honey

½ teaspoon vanilla extract

75 grams frozen diced mango, thawed

120 grams frozen diced pineapple, thawed

¼ cup toasted coconut

Tools

mixing bowl

measuring spoons/scales

spoon

parfait glass or bowl, for serving

1. Combine the Greek yogurt, honey and vanilla extract in a mixing bowl. Set aside.

2. Assemble your parfait by spreading one-third of the yogurt at the bottom of a parfait glass or bowl. Add one-third of the mango and pineapple. Repeat layers until finished.

3. Top with toasted coconut and serve immediately.

Allergen alert!

If you are allergic to dairy, use coconut milk or almond milk yogurt instead of the Greek yogurt.

Coconut is classified as a fruit. But if you have a tree nut allergy, please talk to your doctor before eating it.

CHICKEN NUGGETS
AND AVOCADO DIP

Who doesn't love chicken nuggets? But eggs usually help make the crispy, crunchy nugget coating. Not this time! These crispy bite-sized chicken nuggets and the creamy avocado dip are sure to please your entire family.

Preparation time: 10 minutes

Cooking time: 15 minutes

Serves 4

Ingredients

455 grams boneless, skinless chicken breasts

1 teaspoon kosher salt

½ teaspoon ground black pepper

½ teaspoon garlic powder

½ teaspoon paprika

60 grams plain flour

60 millilitres oil, such as olive oil

Avocado dip

1 avocado

1 lime

½ bunch coriander

1 teaspoon salt

¼ teaspoon hot sauce

Tools

baking tray

baking parchment

chopping board

chef's knife

measuring spoons/scales/jug

bowl

blender

serving dish

Allergen alert!

If you have a wheat allergy, replace the plain flour with a wheat-free flour blend or coconut flour.

1. Preheat oven to 220°C. Line a baking tray with baking parchment and set aside.

2. Carefully cut the chicken into 5-centimetre (2-inch) cubes.

3. Sprinkle the salt, pepper, garlic powder and paprika over all sides of the chicken pieces.

4. In a bowl, roll the chicken in the flour until coated.

5. Place chicken on baking tray, leaving 2.5 centimetres (1 inch) of space between each piece. Drizzle oil over the chicken.

6. Place the baking tray in the oven for about 10 to 15 minutes or until chicken is golden on the outside and no longer pink on the inside.

7. While the chicken bakes, ask an adult to help you peel the avocado and remove its pit. Place the pulp in a blender.

8. Cut the lime in half and squeeze its juice into the blender.

9. Pull the tops of the coriander from the stems and add to blender, along with the salt and hot sauce.

10. Place the lid on the blender. Blend on high until smooth. If the mixture is too thick, add a tablespoon of water and blend again.

11. Pour the dip into a serving dish. Cover and place in refrigerator until served.

12. When the chicken is finished baking, allow to cool five minutes before serving with dipping sauce.

CORN DOG BITES
AND HONEY MUSTARD DIPPING SAUCE

The corn dog is an American favourite – a frankfurter covered in batter and served on a stick. Now you can make an egg-free version with flax and water. It's easy, and the result is a delicious and fun treat!

Preparation time: 20 minutes

Cooking time: 20 minutes

Serves 4

Ingredients

1 tablespoon ground flaxseed

3 tablespoons warm water

120 grams yellow corn meal

125 grams plain flour

2 teaspoons baking powder

1 teaspoon salt

110 grams pure honey

125 millilitres milk

60 millilitres oil, such as olive oil

4 frankfurters

Honey mustard sauce

250 grams coarse ground mustard

170 grams pure honey

1 teaspoon salt

Tools

standard muffin tin

12 muffin cases

2 small bowls

measuring spoons/scales/jug

spoon

large mixing bowl

chopping board

chef's knife

toothpick

1. Preheat oven to 200°C. Line a muffin tin with paper cases and set aside.

2. Combine the flax and warm water together in a small bowl. Stir with a spoon to combine and then let sit for a few minutes.

3. In a large mixing bowl, combine the corn meal, flour, baking powder and salt. Mix well.

4. Add the flax mixture, honey, milk and oil. Stir until combined.

5. Scoop the batter evenly into each muffin cup.

6. Cut each hot dog into three 5-centimetre (2-inch) sections and press a piece into each muffin cup.

7. Bake for about 20 minutes or until a toothpick comes out clean when inserted into the muffin.

8. Make the mustard dipping sauce while the muffins bake. Combine the mustard, honey and salt in a small bowl and stir until mixed.

9. When the muffins are done, allow to cool for about five minutes before serving with the mustard dipping sauce on the side.

Allergen alert!

Coconut flour or almond flour can replace the plain flour to avoid wheat.

Make sure you read labels carefully on your hot dog packages. Soya, dairy or wheat can be hidden in the ingredients list.

Soya milk or almond milk can be used to replace milk.

MINI MEATLOAVES

Meatloaf is a classic American comfort food that is simple to make and yummy to eat. Apple sauce makes these mini meatloaves fluffy, light and absolutely delicious. You won't miss the eggs in this recipe!

Preparation time: 20 minutes

Cooking time: 30 minutes

Serves 4

Ingredients

1 small onion

680 grams lean beef or turkey mince

130 grams apple sauce

1 tablespoon tomato paste

25 grams breadcrumbs

1 teaspoon dried ground thyme

1 teaspoon salt

½ teaspoon ground black pepper

Sauce

120 grams ketchup

60 grams yellow mustard

55 grams dark brown sugar

Tools

baking tray

baking parchment

chopping board

chef's knife

box grater

2 large bowls

measuring spoons/scales/jug

scraper

Allergen alert!

Looking to avoid wheat? Wheat-free breadcrumbs can easily replace the traditional breadcrumbs in this recipe.

1. Preheat oven to 190°C. Line a baking tray with baking parchment. Set aside.

2. Carefully cut the onion in half, and then peel off the skin.

3. Place the box grater on the chopping board. Using the side of the grater with the large holes, gently grate the onion.

4. In a large bowl, combine the beef or turkey, apple sauce, tomato paste, breadcrumbs, thyme, salt, pepper and grated onion.

5. Using clean hands, mix the meat until all of the ingredients are evenly combined.

6. Divide the meat into four equal pieces and form into loaf shapes on the baking tray. Leave at least 5 centimetres (2 inches) of space between each mini loaf.

7. Place the ketchup, mustard and brown sugar in a mixing bowl. Stir to combine.

8. Spread the sauce topping evenly over each loaf using a scraper. Then place the loaves in the oven.

9. Bake for about 30 minutes or until no longer pink inside.

10. Remove from the oven and allow to cool for five minutes before serving hot.

SPINACH-APPLE SALAD

Just like eggs, spinach is a great source of iron. You can create a nutritious and hearty salad with spinach. Get pumped up for this super salad topped with crisp apples and a sweet 'n' tangy dressing!

Preparation time: 15 minutes

Cooking time: 10 minutes

Serves 4

Ingredients

Dressing

60 millilitres apple cider vinegar

125 millilitres extra-virgin olive oil

60 millilitres apple juice

2 tablespoons pure maple syrup

1 tablespoon Dijon mustard

¼ teaspoon salt

¼ teaspoon ground black pepper

Salad

2 Granny Smith apples

120 grams dried cranberries

35 grams sunflower seeds

120 grams fresh spinach leaves

Tools

glass jar with lid

measuring spoons/scales/jug

chopping board

chef's knife

mixing bowl

tongs

1. In a glass jar, combine the cider vinegar, olive oil, apple juice, maple syrup, Dijon mustard, salt and pepper.

2. Screw lid on tightly and shake hard for about 30 seconds or until mixed well. Set aside.

3. Dice the apples into 1.3-centimetre (½-inch) pieces and place in a mixing bowl with the cranberries, sunflower seeds and spinach.

4. Pour three-quarters of the dressing over the salad and toss gently with tongs.

5. Serve on plates with additional dressing on the side.

Allergens eradicated!

No major food allergens found here!

POTATO PANCAKES

Are you a "brinner" person? That's right, go ahead and have breakfast for dinner! Pancakes can be made with lots of different foods, including potatoes. Crispy on the outside, fluffy on the inside, these delicious egg-free cakes are great for any meal!

Preparation time: 10 minutes

Cooking time: 5–10 minutes

Serves 4

Ingredients

2 medium Russet potatoes

60 millilitres olive oil, divided

2 teaspoons salt

1 teaspoon ground black pepper

Tools

vegetable brush

vegetable peeler

chopping board

box grater

medium frying pan

10-cm (4-in) round metal
  biscuit cutter

small juice glass

spatula

tongs

Allergens eradicated!

No major food allergens found here!

1. Scrub the potatoes clean and remove the skin using a vegetable peeler.

2. Place a box grater on a chopping board. Carefully grate the potatoes using the side with large round holes. Divide the grated potatoes into four equal piles and set aside.

3. Place a medium frying pan on the hob set to medium heat. Place the biscuit cutter on the frying pan and pour 1 tablespoon of olive oil inside the cutter.

4. Stuff one of the piles of grated potato inside the cutter. Use the bottom of the juice glass to pack it tightly. Sprinkle with ½ teaspoon salt and ¼ teaspoon pepper.

5. Carefully pull the cutter up and off of the frying pan, leaving the potatoes on the frying pan. Use the tongs to pull off the cutter if it is too hot to touch.

6. Allow to cook about three to five minutes, then gently turn over to cook the other side.

7. Remove the potatoes from frying pan and place on a plate. Cover with foil to keep hot.

8. Repeat steps 3 to 7 for the remaining potatoes.

9. Serve hot as a side dish at breakfast or dinner.

CHEF'S TIP

Top your taters with your favourite condiments: ketchup, salsa or even apple sauce and cinnamon for a sweet treat!

MAPLE-GLAZED CARROTS

You know carrots are good for you, right? But how can you make them pop with flavour? These caramelized carrots will treat your taste buds to a sweet and scrumptious surprise! They are the perfect side to many dishes.

Preparation time: 10 minutes

Cooking time: 20 minutes

Serves 4

Ingredients

450 grams carrots

2 tablespoons oil, such as olive oil

1 teaspoon salt

2 tablespoons pure maple syrup

Tools

baking tray

baking parchment

vegetable peeler

chopping board

chef's knife

measuring spoons/scales/jug

Allergens eradicated!

No major food allergens found here!

1. Preheat oven to 230°C. Line a baking tray with baking parchment and set aside.

2. Peel the carrots with a vegetable peeler. Using a knife, cut the tops off each carrot. Then cut each carrot into 5-centimetre (2-inch) pieces.

3. Place carrots on baking tray and drizzle with oil and salt.

4. Bake in oven for about 10 minutes or until carrots begin to brown.

5. Remove from oven and drizzle with maple syrup.

6. Increase oven temperature to 245°C. Bake an additional five to 10 minutes, or until the carrots have a deep brown colour. Check after five minutes to avoid burning.

7. Serve immediately alongside your main course.

CHEF'S TIP

Sugar and spice make everything nice. Like a little spice? Sprinkle some cayenne pepper (about ¼ teaspoon) over the carrots during step 3.

STRAWBERRY ICE CREAM

Did you know you can combine just four ingredients to make ice cream? Eggs make ice cream rich, but you won't miss them in this sweet summer dessert that can be made or eaten any time of the year.

Preparation time: 10 minutes

Serves 4

Ingredients

450 grams frozen strawberries

1 tablespoon granulated sugar

1 teaspoon almond extract

2 tablespoons coconut cream

Tools

food processor

measuring spoons/scales

spatula

bowls, for serving

Allergen alert!

If you are allergic to nuts, use vanilla extract in place of almond extract.

Coconut is classified as a fruit. But if you have a tree nut allergy, please talk to your doctor before eating it.

1. Place the frozen strawberries, sugar and almond extract in a food processor and pulse it 10 times.

2. Turn the food processor on high until the mix looks as fluffy as soft-serve ice cream.

3. Scrape down the sides of the bowl with the spatula and pour in the coconut cream.

4. Pulse another 5 times and transfer to bowls for serving immediately.

5. Put leftovers in an airtight container in the freezer straight away.

CHEF'S TIP

Substitute blueberries, raspberries or blackberries for the strawberries if you prefer.

COCONUT VANILLA

PUDDING

Are you craving thick, delicious pudding but need to avoid eggs? Creamy and sweet, this delectable pudding can be made for your entire family or scooped into individual servings to take to school in your lunchbox.

Preparation time: 10 minutes
Cooking time: 4 hours (4 hours inactive)
Serves 4

Ingredients

480 millilitres coconut milk

115 grams granulated sugar

3 tablespoons arrowroot powder

2 teaspoons vanilla extract

pinch of kosher salt

Tools

medium saucepan

measuring spoons/scales/jug

whisk

mixing bowl

large bowl, for serving

Allergen alert!

Coconut is classified as a fruit. But if
you have a tree nut allergy, please talk
to your doctor before eating it.

1. Place the coconut milk in a saucepan over medium heat. Bring to a simmer.

2. While the coconut milk heats, combine the remaining ingredients in a mixing bowl.

3. When the milk begins to simmer, slowly pour the sugar mixture into the saucepan, whisking while pouring to dissolve.

4. Continue to stir gently until the mixture begins to thicken.

5. Pour pudding into a serving bowl. Chill for at least four hours before serving.

6. Store leftovers in an airtight container in the refrigerator for up to one week.

CHEF'S TIP

Top the pudding with your favourite
fruits or cookie pieces for extra flavour!

LEMON CUPCAKES

Skipping cake because of the eggs? Think again! You can enjoy the cake you've been dreaming of, just without the eggs. Slightly sweet and tart to your tongue, these cupcakes are sure to please.

Preparation time: 15 minutes

Cooking time: 25 minutes

Serves 12

Ingredients

cooking spray

250 grams plain flour

225 grams caster sugar

pinch of kosher salt

2 teaspoons baking powder

125 millilitres oil

240 millilitres milk (any kind)

2 lemons

Icing

2 lemons

65 grams icing sugar

Tools

standard muffin tin

2 mixing bowls

measuring spoons/scales/jug

wooden spoon

box grater

chopping board

chef's knife

toothpick

small mixing bowl

fork

Allergen alert!

Are you trying to avoid wheat?
Wheat-free flour blend can replace
the plain flour in this recipe.

1. Preheat oven to 180°C. Lightly spray a muffin pan with cooking spray. Set aside.

2. Combine the flour, sugar, salt and baking powder in a large mixing bowl. Set aside.

3. Combine the oil and milk in a second bowl. Set aside.

4. Rinse the lemons. Carefully zest the outer yellow part of the rind using the side of the box grater with the small round holes. Add the zest to the oil and milk mixture.

5. Cut 2 lemons in half and squeeze the juice into the oil and milk mixture. Be careful to avoid seeds. Stir to combine.

6. Add the wet ingredients to the dry ingredients and mix well.

7. Fill each muffin cup two-thirds full. Bake for 20 to 25 minutes or until a toothpick inserted into the centre comes out clean.

8. Make the glaze while the cupcakes bake. Cut 2 lemons in half and squeeze the juice into a mixing bowl.

9. Add the icing sugar and mix with a fork until dissolved.

10. Remove the cupcakes from the oven and allow to cool completely. After the cupcakes have cooled, remove them from the pan and drizzle the icing evenly over the tops.

11. Store leftovers in an airtight container for up to one week.

GLOSSARY

assemble put all the parts of something together

blend mix together, sometimes using a blender

consume eat or drink something

dissolve incorporate a solid food into a liquid by melting or stirring

drizzle let a substance fall in small drops

mash smash a soft food into a lumpy mixture

pit single central seed or stone of some fruits

pulp soft juicy or fleshy part of a fruit or vegetable

simmer keep just below boiling when cooking or heating

slice cut into thin pieces with a knife

thaw bring frozen food to room temperature

whisk stir a mixture rapidly until it's smooth

zest scrape off the thin outer peel of a citrus fruit for use as flavouring

READ MORE

Allergy-free Cooking for Kids, Pamela Clark (Sterling Epicure, 2014)

The Allergy-Free Family Cookbook, Fiona Heggie and Ellie Lux (Orion, 2015)

The Kids Only Cookbook, Sue Quinn (Quadrille Publishing, 2013)

WEBSITE

www.allergyuk.org

If you have any allergies, this is the website to go to. It provides lots of useful information and a helpline.